FRESH SUCCESS QUOTES

Johny Einstein & Chatram Trivedi

Amazon

The fresh collection is taken from the real life and dedicated to every incident which contirbuted to it.

INTRODUCTION

The book will take you through every word selected from the life and motivates you in attaining the success in every way you want from it.

PREFACE

The book will surely motivate to the reader which will surely bring success to them if they really absorb in their life.

JOHNY EINSTEIN

Fresh Success Quotes

"Success never create second thought".

"Success follows me because they know my attitude".

"Success is a gift of parent's blessings".

"Uncountable steps brings success near to you".

JOHNY EINSTEIN

"Success always bow in front of patience".

" 'Positive attitude' is the main ingredients
of a dish called success".

"Only one person in the world can motivate
me for success, and it's me".

"Your negative remarks cannot defeat my positive efforts for success".

JOHNY EINSTEIN

"Success cannot be enjoyed with successful people but with those who are seriously trying for it".

"Bullet of failure cannot puncture my goal for success".

16

" 'Fresh wind' and 'Amazing morning' always motivates me, how successful life looks like".

"Sharing a success always bring more success to your life".

JOHNY EINSTEIN

"Success is colorless but It can make your world colorful".

"For me success is contributing to the society".

"Success cannot be measured in money or position but only in self-satisfaction".

"Throughout the journey I never met success
but only beautiful moments".

JOHNY EINSTEIN

"When success meets success it creates jealousy,
when effort meets effort it creates success".

"When I totally broke down, success told me you are still not done".

"Tough situations are potential creator of success".

"Lottery wins by luck, success comes by strong desire to get it".

JOHNY EINSTEIN

32

"The best perfume in the world is success".

"When efforts are matchless, rest things
are obligation even success".

"Teach me how to become skillful not the successful".

"Failure can be experienced long lasting as compare to success".

" I'm habitual to complete tough job, I don't know when success comes and go in between ".

"Do you know the secret of success, do it by yourself".

41

"True success means when you become mentor
for others who are trying for it".

BOOKS BY THIS AUTHOR

Fresh Success Quotes, Motivating Business Quotes , Golden Quotes Of Life

All the books give a deep thought in your life and will change it drastically in a positive way.

CHANGE

I request every reader to forward this book and creative thinking of author not for profit but in order to bring good change in the society for every beautiful reasons.

www.ingramcontent.com/pod-product-compliance
Lightning Source LLC
Chambersburg PA
CBHW061025250726
48662CB00011B/2100